WAITRESS IN FALL

Waitress in Fall

KRISTÍN ÓMARSDÓTTIR

— POEMS —

selected & translated from the Icelandic by

VALA THORODDS

PARTUS PRESS

MMXX

First co-published by Carcanet Press and Partus Press in 2018. This revised second edition published by Partus Press in 2020.

Partus Press Ltd
266 Banbury Road
Oxford OX2 7DL
United Kingdom

www.partus.press

A CIP catalogue record for this book is available from the British Library, ISBN 9781913196042.

Design & composition: Studio Lamont. Printed in Estonia.

CONTENTS

We may keep the home fire burning,
or we may burn the house down;
we may stay home, burning inwardly,
or we may take off in a conflagration
of self-assertion. We watch the fires
of destruction, of desire, and of
ambition, and wonder what we can
risk, and what we might gain.

LAUREN ELKIN, *Flâneuse*

Like fire that burns the field, prepares
it for crops, let the mind be seared by
failure into readiness.

SASHA WEST, 'Agriculture Begins'

from

OUR HOUSE IS FULL
OF FOG

★

(*Í húsinu okkar er þoka*)

1987

RUNNER GIRL

I'm a runner girl
and the dusk lives
in my eyes.

I
make advances on the night.

My lips
drink sweat
and thirst;

my lips,
gentle gentle,

my lips,
lovely lovely.

*

My tongue is skilled
and knows how to capsize minds;
so if you've thoughts,
like stones like spears,
they'll slide down the valley
– straight into the sea!
And never never walk
again
crouched
inside you.

*

My mouth is a mussel.
My cunt tastes like a prawn.

Breasts white and soft
like fish cheeks.

My legs are sprigs
– always wiggling!

*

I'm a brand-new runner girl
with fire in the pit of my stomach
and my knees in stitches.

Completely newgrown
– grew up last year!

Dad calls me a flower
and mum doesn't understand a thing.

No!
I am not a dry doughnut
you eat with milk.
I'm a mussel,
prawn and fish cheek.
– A new potato in fall
buttered, with salt.

Skin ice-cold milk;
sometimes tepid
sometimes steamed.

*

And my nostrils
dog-like
sniff you
and sniff you out.

– I know where we will be found –

GARDEN IN A METROPOLIS

I.

The rain grows.
It echoes under the trees.
The tick-trickling stream
whispers a magnitude to the ears.
The air hums and
rubber lances swish
going down,
down underground.

The rain grows.
On the endless silence of man.
No god not a soul
under the curtain of trees.
Above us is the river,
might and ocean
– there sail kayaks and rafts.
Above us is the river
– Ophelia on three wings
bathes herself
and rolls slowly to one side.

Our mud-caked journey
down a narrow path.
The rain grows.
The boles strike at my heart.
– You sniff out my every step.
The boles strike at my heart.
You are a wild animal,
suffocate me
but lose
if I lay down
on the ground.

II.

Familiar tigers in heat in cages
– nearby but nowhere.
Native ceremonies hidden under trees.
The trucks of the city ascend the sky.
Through the narrow glades
I beware of you
but call to you
in silence.

Your eyes those of the bird
say:
– do something! –
And I rush into the greenery,
never look at you again.

III.

We'll tiptoe
into green disasters.
Your eyes wet.

Dig up out of each other
the cries of the animal.

The rain grows
under the leaf crowns.

I stretch your lips.
You colour my cheeks.
Drink the fear in my eyes.

Who are you
Who are you

IV. *Tongue and Silence*

i.

You sprinkle sawdust
on my silence.
On my wet dripping wet
silence

sawdust.

ii.

Your tongue,
long long,
washes me onto dry
land, into a valley:

    and everything is merry
    with us.

    You speak
    and I.

iii.

I pour from my cunt
the dripping goldveins of kings:

    behold,
    that you disappear,
    my friend,
    behold you disappear,
    my bird friend.

iv.

I scan your cavity
and try to hear
your heart stir.

      You are the silence
      in heat, and full
      of shouts made of smooth velvet.

v.

My heart beats
in your palm
and only there.

It bursts!
in your palm
– only there.

*

Anoint my sleep
and breast
with your tongue

and promises
of cautious
fingers.

*

And praise me!
say:
– you do well –

and praise me!
into sleep
into sleep
with you:

– that I do not walk
woodlands
searching for you,

with you – .

Come closer,
take my head
too!

give my
thought a hand,
touch my tenderness,

and praise me!
and permit me
to sleep
under you.

vi.

I touch a murmur, and
move slightly.
You lay me
a life buoy.

Murmur, and a skinny
cable
quivering
and still within earshot
– a whimper.

     ★

Birds kept vigil
over us
and still I wake
inside you.

And follow you
to mountains and
home pastures
hidden under a wing.

But only
for a brook's babble
and hollow,
tongue and throat.

vii.

May your tongue, longer than
another, wash me ashore.

That I be able to speak and
utter mud from my lips.

     *

Pitch-black solariums
of an ancient morning blush

and bubbles, soap bubbles
burst at your window

and you wait
lying with burned fingers:

      ancient, drudging
      candlelight
      and locked doors.

That I be able to speak
and your windows be adorned
with vines and blue
spruce and you weave
me in nets and
undress,
caress and lick
my slimy flesh
and the heat fog of your

house wipes out the slog in
the puddles of oblivion and
in the morning breeze:
fingerprints
and words.

viii.

Go out and defend myself.

First a fence post,
then string,

barbed wire, nails
and more sticks.

– This is our
place, here
we were – .

Send a message
and after you, a horse

     come and see
     our story
     a fort
     above ground

ix.

See I hang
upright on a cliff

and my poem,
a whittled note,

and my poem,
a paper airplane,
a boat made of paper,

    it floats
    on a pond
    by your
    lodgings

from

WAITRESS AT
AN OLD RESTAURANT

★

(*þerna á gömlu veitingahúsi*)

1993

THE WHITE DOVES

The doves at home
are white as sails.
Yet I have told no one about them.

They play curtains when I sleep
and curtains while I wake.

My love, if I die.

EVENT

tied to a deck chair
inside a mountain
with a warm clock
in my mouth

every quarter hour

    a strike

from above

and pennies
pelt
the back of my neck

from the slot

drops

LOVER

like a jar
he waits for him

for him to draw near

waits for him
like a jar

DOMESTIC PEACE

three children lick milk
from the trees
the mother sits in a bamboo
chair and crochets hearts together

the father comes home
as the sun drops
with white birds on his back

leaves behind heavy
spoors
in the road

the mother sweeps them over
and the foxes go blind

no one enters this place
without permission

THREE POETESSES

Three poetesses
in white bras
sit around a low
round-table.
With books in hand.

A man dressed in a pirate sweater
comes in through the door
from a snowstorm and sits
at the women's table.

Takes off his sweater.

When he touches
one of them
they are already dead.
And don't come back to life.
Though they await his kisses.

Then he stands up,
takes hold of the touched one
and carries her out.

The current of air
when the door opens and closes
turns the pages of the books
of all three.

ON A HOT DAY

swarming with blind
old
doe rabbits
in the chair

lap up the words
I left behind
on the three-legged
table in the garden

when I approach
barefoot
with earmuffs
and a furry rifle

LOVER X:

I put on a pair of gloves
(lead grey)
and embraced you.

I snapped on a mask
(leather)
and spoke to you.

With a wig I departed
for town
to meet others.

> (you were taking a bath,
>   give me a moment, I always get
>   hysterical when I
>   think about you
>   in the bathtub, just a moment)

And I returned home with
a pearl-trimmed heart.
(sewed it myself)
Long nails.
(of course I counted the days)
Red lips
in the left and right palm:

> give me treats
> treat me good

they said to you on the doorstep
as I returned.

WAITRESS IN FALL

she wipes the blood from her face
(the sword)
rinses the apron in the cold cold water
(in the blue sink)
lays down the apron

the morning dew demands an answer
in order to dry

walks out

    *

whether she murdered, was murdered
doesn't matter

    *

the autumn air is tender on the foothills
clear as water in a truthpond

the morning dew rests
against her blue cheek

DREAM

a mother returns

with an apron round her waist
holds a silent
tray

returns

pretzels
hot
breadsnails

crawl up

the rim

returns

golden butter!

her hips clean
her eyes equally blue

returns

the fragrant luggage

REGARDS

1.

the fish in my sink
loves coffee
I send it down
with loving regards

2.

a bird on the roof sings
as soon as I light the papers
people gather together
outside

3.

but the front door died
when the bicycle abandoned me

4.

in the bathroom cries
a frog
in my white lace
handkerchief

in the evenings like a church choir,
in the mornings a knitting machine
producing scarves

5.

I send it down
with loving regards

LOVER X:

My jug full of blue water
and suns.
I knew I would burn
that's why I didn't partake of it.
Not until the moon
dug itself under the fjord
and the snow.
Then I warmed myself up.
With blue water and suns.

*

Had been alone longer than I suspected
and dusted off the tablecloth.
No tracks in the snow,
the road gone off with a ship.
The tablecloth orange coloured sometimes.
And the gate fixed to the sky.
Had been alone longer than I suspected
tending to my tasks.

My jug full of blue water
awaited me at the table.
And as I swept the floors I looked over there.
At the suns floating down and up.
I swept and cocked my eyes.
At my jug that was full of
blue water and suns.
The water in the tap awaited me no longer.

*

You know I won't abandon you.
Though you'll come no closer I won't abandon you.

*

Silence inside, silence outside.
In hard snow and broken sky.
When the moon crashes.

Into the ocean that had frozen over
longer ago than I suspected.

SUMMER'S DAY

a tree on a stand in my garden
and children's hats on poles
line up
around it

the coffee pot arrives
from the blue house
when I call
from the old chair

the wind emits a sound
but can't be seen or touched
the laundry in its place on the clothesline
duvet covers and sheets, and the sun

the hats walk around
the tree

I clap for an encore
the coffee pot pours from itself
into the mug

hooray!
hooray!

from the old chair

UNCHAINED

the cadets carry me to their home
drag me out of my clothes
hang them up on a hook
and laugh

at last,
I think, privately

they dress me in military blue
and cut off my hair
paint a red wound on my breast

'now you play a wounded cadet
behind enemy lines, onto the stretcher
with you!'

they carry me through the streets
laughing cadets
and the screaming children
triumphant

at last,
I think, privately

at last
I am free

THE NIGHT CALLS

on her cavalry

to follow her
give her red blood
for the cloths
so her old night rags
don't unravel
this winter

instead she offers them

    nightmilk!
    nightmilk!

from the taps of the car parks
from the taps of the house walls
gardens
alleyways
under the pond bridge
by the parking meters
pier stilts
nightmilk from near and far
wherever thirst is ignited
nightmilk

from bursting taps
fire hydrants
press one button
and the cheerful nightmilk streams
onto your
face

    nightmilk!
    nightmilk!

WAITRESS AT AN OLD RESTAURANT

she rubs your table
hands you the menu

the clocks tick in your pockets
tick for you

she is faceless
but you lend her a face from the lineage
of your father
no one has used it in a long time

the clocks strike your thighs
strike your thighs:

you stand up
take hold of her
carry her out

the clock in the hall strikes a heavy
sentencing blow
on your shoulder:

you have freed
the queen herself
who cries out

from here on out
all roads are open to you

from

CLOSE YOUR EYES
AND THINK OF ME

*

(*Lokaðu augunum og hugsaðu um mig*)

1998

FIRE

As beautiful as the irons in the smithy
in the old dark that was
your eyes
when they pursue, accuse and finally
move me
like a container that turns into a bird
that flies into a fire that is
hot

away

(and we anoint palmsoft
oil
onto the tonguetip)

As beautiful as air
in an old church that,
patient, looks upon the day-long
quiet guests year after year
come in
your eyes await
another fire

ADDRESS

Does the moon have an address or not.
It is punctual, it is always in the same spot.
But is it like my lips on a long journey.

THE WATERMELON AND ME

Your hands and fingers, as I forget not
the fingers though I mention the hands, enjoy the confidence
of the tomatoes, the peppers, the chilli, the leek,
the Chinese parsley, and of me.

The watermelon will not abandon your lips
when you eat and neither will I.

The watermelon will not abandon your lips.
Neither will I.

STOVE

I dreamt I gave you a kitchen stove.
Unearthly and beautiful kitchen stove.
The stove that everyone dreams of but no one attains.

Its buttons told you everything.
The oven held the deeps that no one sees and the bright flames.
The warming drawer was the warming drawer of a winner.

I carried the stove into your room and placed it by the window.
So the taste of the expanse and the taste of our isolation would meet

in the pots themselves.

MORNING GIFT

The socks are here.

The thread stretches and the thread disappears.
The thread is unyielding and the thread holds nothing.
The thread is blasé and the thread is ablaze.

The socks are here.
I bring them to you with the red dress.

WISH

The day that I don't wake up
I wish
that someone will be close by.
Someone who knows my body.

WOOL HEART

Though I talk a lot I crave silence about my life.
In the foreground of my life sits you.
To you I bring the words that my life drives away.
And all I have and all that I have yet to have.
In sleep I live for myself but in waking I live for others.
More precisely:
in sleep my heart counts down.
In waking my heart is made of wool and there inside I keep your
    palm.

THE FATALISTIC POEM

Your hands and fingers are bells that ring
but one day they will not jingle inside me
like they have (countless times) before
and they will not ring like bells
but the grass will be mown by their sound.

The last sentence has been written before.
I throw it out there like everything else, my love.

This day I look upon the pack of horses,
observe the enchanting behinds that though and yet
are graced
with tails
such fine ones
getting farther away from my house.

Which won't be bigger than my house today, but more remote.
Like a lifetime. You know how that side of things goes, my love.

And I will miss the decorations in the back
but I won't cry for help though you are one of the ones that leave.
When the direction is the sunset, the blessed direction is the
    sunset, what is one to do?

I won't wait up.

I drape myself in a blanket and maybe the blanket gives me a tail.
A lucky, lovely tail when I wake up.

A tail that adorns that which opens and refuses to close.

Because, like safe-deposit boxes open and open and open
in the hands of thieves, thus am I.
I open and don't close.
Thus are you.
You open and don't close.

At this turning point I therefore grow a tail
for that which opens and completely refuses to close.

You remember where I read you this poem for the first time?

*On the steps in front of the old factory in the sunset and you were drunk
thinking of breaking up with me. (We had slept together a total of five
nights, this is how good I am at counting.) With the poem I proved that
I had known beforehand that you were thinking of breaking up with me.
You gave it a name and opened my eyes to the literal and conservative
arrogance of it. Best to keep the literal and conservative arrogance going
a little longer:*

The morning that you and the horses desert me
you spend under their protection and brush and brush your hair.

Secretly monitor my eyes that overtly monitor you
and your much, much brushed hair.
While the ponytails of the horses scythe the dark green grass.

Then you leave. The direction is the sunset.
And I have to try everything in order to wake up
and draw forth from my reticule
bells
that will ring in your ears your journey to its end.

PROTEIN

I see to it that my man has the guts and the vigour to love me.

Rice, potatoes, and eggs never fail me.

I put some of these in a pan or a pot and when dusk falls he lies in my arms.

Wherever we go I think first and foremost of food.

When we eat together I make a wish that I were a dove and he were a dog and after the meal I have my wish fulfilled.

I tiptoe along his sated body until I get my portion of the workings of the energy wad.

From morning till night I look forward to the moment when he squirts into me the fluid that I do all I can to co-produce.

I worship every hour of the day because each is preparation for this marvellous moment.

But sometimes my heart (my dove heart) decides and demands rest and then I drink him.

Milk, water, fruit juice with ice, none of this has as good an effect on the mucous membrane.

Or the skin of the face.

Or the hair.

But then I'm back to where I started because I stand over the pots in the house of my sister and act indifferent as her friends peek into the kitchen to examine me.

They never prepare food, they don't have any boyfriends.

The skin on their faces has long since lost its softness.

They stare at my red hair and admire its cultivation.

I say nothing, I just smile, am polite and continue milling about the pots.

My sister loves me but her love doesn't need kisses or food.

DESSERT

When I sit at the dinner table I look at three men who have sucked
my breasts.
One sucks them still, two sucked them temporarily.
I look at the sun flooding in through the window and I look at the
glasses on the table.
I look at three mouths that open and close around the food.
I look at the food disappear from the table as the sun shifts in the
window.
I say:

You have all sucked my breasts.

As they wipe their mouths with the napkins.

They nod and smile at me and I smile at them.

The meal is not over, I add. There is dessert.
I say and stand up because I don't want anyone to leave.

I want to have my eyes closed as I bring them the dessert.
The hot, red-hot dessert and whipped cream.

LEMON BREAST

In the summer it is best to have lemon breast
in the afternoon indoors near
an open window.

Slice the lemon into two equal halves
on the kitchen table but take
one half into your room
and squeeze a little of the liquid
over the brown
soft
half-asleep
nipple.

Lick up the drops that trickle down the breast
before the lips are moved
to the top.

Lick first then suck.

When the taste fades
repeat.

TRADITION

In the shelter of night, men escort women to the hospital.
Whether it's on foot, in a cab, their own or a borrowed car.
In the lightfaint corridor of the hospital the man sits down on a
    bench or in a chair while the orderly takes the woman in to see
    the doctor.
There the doctor listens to the woman's words and heartbeat.
Or goes into her and takes a test.
Meanwhile the man sits in the corridor and chats to the night
    guard.
Sometimes the man and the night guard drink coffee from plastic
    cups but mostly the man drinks the coffee from the plastic cup
    alone.
Before daybreak the doors to the examination room open and
    the man escorts the woman farther down the passages of the
    hospital.

On the girl in the red coat's shoulder sits a dove
(grey).
On her other shoulder, a black raven.

The dove has a spiderweb over its eyes
and the raven is crying
because it doesn't have
a spiderweb covering its eyes and in its stomach
is nothing but dust.

Why is there nothing but dust in the raven's stomach?

Because the girl gives it nothing to eat.
The dove's stomach is full of popcorn
because the girl went to the cinema last Saturday
(ravens don't eat popcorn).

Then the girl walks down Laugavegur and gets hit
by a yellow car in Lækjargata.

Why was she hit by a yellow car in Lækjargata?

On account of the coherence of the colour choice:
red coat, black raven, grey dove
yellow car
spiderweb
popcorn
and
dust.

The fly loves the flower and the flower adorns nature with its
climax.

A mother adorns her sorrow with a thin handkerchief that she
refuses to get wet, that she cannot bring herself to get wet,
that is woven in a way not dissimilar to the way in which the
spider crochets her livelihood.

This is how I want to wound the language.

The knives in the kitchens of single women who order a lot of takeaway sorely need whetting. The knives in the knife block are of no use to the bread crust or the proud tomatoes or the patient onion of the woman who unwittingly brings unprepared food into the kitchen of a woman who stops cooking when her lovers disappear.

Their impossible knives, completely impossible knives, neglected and dusty, in obtrusive kitchens that only get plugged in if he who can return the proteins into the abdomen of the kitchen's owner is nearby.

Still, the gardens display their finest. The lemons on the trees await the hands that will squeeze them over the old asparagus. And the redcurrants spread over everything like inebriated lanterns, though that reminds me mostly of the kisses we didn't repeat.

And still it is also magnificent to slice vegetables into the stomach of one's love with a sharp knife slice and slice vegetables and again vegetables with a sharp knife into the stomach of one's love slice and slice the vegetables down with a sharp knife. Into the stomach of one's love.

Lovely unloved women, you who open the door to young delivery boys bearing lukewarm, fertile, plastic tubs of food, some in uniform, some in their own clothes but all with the waking young eyes that touch anything in their path, whet the knives in your kitchens, whet them.

GIFT

Some people who are already grown need to cry like children.
Once a week, every two months, a few times a year.
Then it's good to create the conditions that bring forth those tears.
Wrong them or leave them behind.

RAIN DAYS

I want to tell you about the dim rain days.
When the rain streams in and the girls that love me
can't work fast enough to keep it from the threshold
and the shadows' wishes for bodies come true.

About the rain days that give men and vegetation life.

The dead one ceases to be dead if only the rain fills her hearing.
Like unfamiliar boots at the bedside, like water
to the water bucket, so is the rain to the corpse.

I want to talk about the long dim endless rain days
when I walk in the circles intended for me, from kitchen
to foyer into the bedroom and from there to the living room
out into the hall on the other side to the kitchen while the girls
    battle the rain
outside the door and the shadows get their wishes fulfilled.

The dead one ceases to be lonely and the heavy scent of the trees
is borne in through the open window if these days last into summer
which in fact happens often.

Tell you about the sloshing rain days with the writhing stream
that never stops. Like a childhood that, unresentful and happy,
cuts its ties with the course of nature.

Long and dim, long and dim days when no one awaits anything.

The embossed shadows and air that tastes like the spirit of a
    sleeping dog
to which the girls' faraway splashing adds a whole lot of exuberance.

Long and dim and soft and tired rain days.

ONE DAY

One day I wake up and need to be taken from behind.
Undress, my shirt unbuttoned button by button.
Under your disinterested eyes and offer you my body.
Throw it on the fire.

The camera that takes pictures of your lungs loves you but you
    don't notice its love.
Actually, yes. When you took off your shirt and your skin touched
    for the first time the mirror-smooth steel, then you noticed its
    love but forgot it immediately.
The women behind the camera love you too.
And the developing machine.
And the light that illuminates the new x-ray of your lungs.
The finger of the doctor.
The lines, the darkness, and the fog that make up the image.
They love you.
But you just aren't ready yet.

The woman whose husband refuses to love has beautiful legs.

Her legs walk across the square in clean tights.

The woman also has a bag and is wearing a green jacket on her stroll.

Her lovers are me, three boys, and an old woman.

We sit by the square in trousers.

The old woman is actually wearing such a long coat that it can't be seen whether she's wearing a dress or trousers but at least it's clear that she's not blind when the woman with the beautiful legs walks across the square and heads towards her door.

Her mysterious door to her even more mysterious office.

I imagine she takes off her clean tights and puts on another pair of clean tights once she's inside, and hangs the first pair up in her window by the square.

For us, her lovers.

MANY PAIRS OF EYES

Alternately you look into my eyes and at my breasts.
I look into your eyes and look at you looking at my breasts.
My breasts look at your trouser pockets.
Your trouser pockets contain your hands.
The buttons on your trouser pockets are falling asleep.
They wake to the sound of the alarm clock.
The alarm clock doesn't ring right away.

MOOD

The nipples of the batteries soften my eyes tonight.
Tonight I will love.
You.

from

SPECIAL DAY

★

(Sérstakur dagur)

2000

POEM ABOUT GOOD GIRLS

Good girls pat you on the back in the dairy aisle of the grocery
    store because they want to comfort and encourage you.
Good girls give you money for chocolate when you are penniless
    and hungry.
Good girls talk about the good weather in good weather and the
    bad weather in bad weather.
Good girls see virtue where there is virtue and vice where there
    is vice.
Good girls know how to get ready for bed. They take their clothes
    off in a certain order.
First the socks.
Good girls never boast about dirty toes.
Nextfirst the sweater.
Thereafter the skirt or trousers.
The underwear always last.
Good girls fuck with benevolence and cry at the end of intercourse.
Good girls never sniff their own socks, only the socks of others.
That way they can be a source of good.
Good girls stroke your hair late at night.
Good girls give their mums books about good people.
Good girls say to their mums:
Mum, let's be good to each other.
Good girls are crybabies in secret.
Good girls.
Hopefully their depiction here is clear and ominous.
Good girls.
Relish God's gifts and brush their teeth afterwards.
Good girls.
Just beware of me.

LAIN UNDER TREES

the leaves on the trees
printed letters
stamped claws
shillings in the sky
strings of pearls that don't reach me

MIRROR

his light is always equally old and equally new
you are its interval

GREEN GRASS

Sports arenas and graveyards take up equal amounts of space in
    the world.
That is an invariable rule.

The grass-grown sports fields.
The grass-grown burial grounds.

Wriggling feet on the ground.
And feet that can't move, in the ground.
Under the heavy duvet.
Green grass.

If a square metre of green grass is reserved for sport
a square metre of green grass is allocated for death.

Who said anyway that our basement was empty?
What nonsense, it's packed full of corpses.
Men who died yesterday.
That lie down on top of the men that died the day before.

We all meet in the end.
In the bunk beds underground.
As we spread the sportsduvet over us.

    *

'Oh how sweet it is mummy to have such a warm duvet
under the nice green shagpile that the gardener grooms.'

'Hush hush, quiet now,
the square metres that go into cheering and crying and the
    gnashing of teeth
demand as many square metres of silence.
Hush.
My child.
It's just as nice to sleep under green turf
as to be an athlete above ground.
Because then you don't need a hat when it rains.'

*

Thus the balance of nature and human life is indisputable.

how do you say *I miss you* in a language that no one in the world understands. I want to speak this language. that it be given to me and one other person. no one else. maybe it will happen that other day. like so often something unexpected happens here on earth. and the sentence will sound once and for all. *yours I.*

HEADLESS MORNING

early one morning you receive in the post
the head of a man
damp with blood
on the doorstep

like the milk here before
like the morning papers of days gone by
like the letters in the envelopes

and the sound of a car engine grows distant

who wishes me ill?
you think at the same time as you
finger your neck

the sun and the morning songs of the birds
empty what's left of the consciousness

THE STAGE BY THE RAINBOW

you there shooting old lipsticked doves
in tiny dollshoes with a heel

you trying on the shoes

this shoe is impossible
this one
fine

you in new doveshoes with the sky on a string

hey!

ANOTHER STAGE BY THE RAINBOW

I flog you
but as you know, that means so many things
we sit in the empty auditorium
or are you the stage and I the stalls
or the other way round
and if we hold hands there is something in our palms that stings
perhaps a needle from an old heart
perhaps a syringe
perhaps a thorn from an old witch
perhaps an eerie feeling
you are the seat and I am the sitter
or the other way round
and on the stage sits an old married couple with a ball
gymnastics class at the old folks' home or what
no
let's turn this around
I do a somersault, you catch the body parts
and stand with them in your arms triumphant
within the applause

flog me again

FIVE CENTIMETRES

the space between death and life is five centimetres
the space between breast and abdomen
the space between sight and hearing
the space between love and affection
the space between sarcasm and laughter
the space between a fever and its absence
the space between you and me
the space between us loving one another and not loving one
    another
the space between sleep and waking
the space between father and son, mother and daughter and siblings
the space between me and you
the space between liquid and matter
the space between me waking you and you lulling me to sleep
the space between us making love and us dressing
the space between despair and hope
the space between me calling and you answering
the space between past and future
the space between happiness and sadness
the space between you opening your mouth and me listening
the space between you and me
the space between hand and arm
the space between thought and action
the space between silence and sound
the space between male lovers
the space between eyes and words
the space between me waking you up and you falling asleep
the space between Sunday and Monday
the space between me and you now

SCISSORS

cut a piece from the eyelid of a son or daughter
and sew into one's eyelids

cut a piece of a young female arse and add to
an older male arse

cut a piece from a lip and put in a secret place
on the body where few will find it

cut, exchange nipples

old gets a new one, new gets an old one
a son gets a father's, a mother a son's

put the spare nipple
of a deceased friend or animal
on one buttock

open possibilities in communication
grapple about things
grow together not apart

no end

from

CHRISTMAS POEMS

*

(*Jólaljóð*)

2006

CHRISTMAS SNOW

Some call it sugar.
Santa Claus's icing sugar
as he sieves the fresh snow
from the clouds down onto
the cake.

Then the residents see the prints
towards the house and the prints
from the house.

Who came, who went.
Who neither came nor went.

Fun to be the first
to imprint the cake.

NIGHTPOEM OF THE WASHER-UP

When the neighbours' lights go out
I hang up the dishwashing brush
on a nail and put on pyjamas.

Turn down the radiator, turn off the lights,
open the window: the dreamgate,
lock the front door, check the doorknob.

And behold, punctually the doors
of the sleep palace open, in
walks an unconfirmed daughter.

APPLEMILK

at three in the morning go into the kitchen

pour milk into a glass, take out a red apple
or green and sit down at the table

eat the apple, drink the milk

and the context of existence
that the poets seek
is found

QUATRAIN

on my stomach I lay
and sensed well
the wings on my back
quivering with desire

SNOWFALL (I)

Fun to draw with a white crayon
on coloured paper each snowflake
that comes to earth.
Each and every one.

The snowflakes come to earth.

Soothing cotton on the eardrum.

Old raindrops that want to be seen,
hide the ground, lay a blanket over the ground.

Spread a sheet over the furniture.

Hide the people in the people themselves.

VERSE

the aroma of the cognac
rocks the head like a
pond rocks a boat

the head is loosed from its
home port and heads for
the deep

CHRISTMAS PSALM

The snowflakes that fall from heaven
play notes hidden in the grass.
We find our footing in an invisible
soundforest.

from

SEE YOUR BEAUTY

★

(*Sjáðu fegurð þína*)

2008

GUIDANCE

Every step of the way the poet follows the tour guide
who enlightens a group of curious cagouled tourists
searching for spiritual exhaustion in the winter cold
before luncheon is served;
whale meat on a bed of ice.

'Now the poets no longer sit in cafés
and drink hot chocolate and eat 'Napoleon's hat' buns
as in times past. But should your feet lead you
into the department stores, use the opportunity, breathe deeply,
and discern what your nose discovers
until every other scent disappears
and what remains is the putrid stench of a long-dead poet.'

The tour guide smiles and points to the poet
who bows nobly.
The onlookers clap their hands.
The applause raises the temperature on this frosty morning;
the mountain veiny with ice, threaded with ice seams.
What will be said of this later?

On a red sheet I rest under a duvet decorated with pink flowers and green leaves. An orange sweater on the sofa next to a blue shirt. Substitutes, sleeping shadows.

Grass-green socks lie on the floor. A pair of severed feet that drank in the colour of the field and fell asleep.

But aren't the flowers in the purple vase on the table called tulips?

The shoes are gone. Where did they go? Followed the cadets that marched by late last night drunk on kisses and wine?

While the stars carved see-through patterns on the windowpanes. Carved see-through patterns in my palm with a glass cutter.

And the moon shadowed the eyelids with silver.
The dark poured itself in through the window.

The day takes off its make-up.
A red pillow on top of a yellow sofa.

I lay a silver-haired head on the pillow. Severed.
Next to an orange sweater, blue shirt.

AUTUMNAL SOUP

rainwater into a pot
yellow leaves with red berries
onion, skull
simmer

The colour of the dirt is browner than velvet and so deep that the eyes dive into it like a star swimmer into a plunge pool. Along the slope the shrubs grow slowly and shoot down tentative roots, ready to take off. Like a smartly dressed violinist waiting for the conductor to send a limousine.

Red gravel forms the first stretch of path up the mountain, where the bride and groom go to track down the desperation that stimulates their intimate caresses. A father and son go this same way to negotiate peace. The deep-voiced breeze whispers:
'Peace. Peace. Be with you.'

The trail is also trodden by brothers longing for their teen years. With packed lunches from their wives who wait at home with the dinner and hopeful tenderness and tissues in their apron pockets.

And there go claustrophobic women, heavy footed and stubborn with fear. Blinded by the produce of the grapevine, in the hopes of reclaiming their sight, because the view distorts the suffering.

Female relatives who share a fiancé sit down on the mountain crest, find dice in their backpacks and throw:
'He is mine, he is mine. He is yours, he is yours…'
But they don't care who gets him. Chance rules the throw.

And on top of the mountain Vikings search for runaway slaves to wash their swords in. For slave girls to wash their spears in. But don't see a girl who is missing her national-costume doll, a pencil case, her swimming stuff, and the pink comb.

East of the gravel path sits your mother on a grassy slope and looks evening-tired over the countryside. There you can pick dandelions, bluebells, buttercups, sea mayweed, forget-me-nots, sheep's sorrel; and soon the berries will be ripe.

Your sweetheart lies in the back seat of the car and sleeps while you stand by the bonnet and talk on the phone under a few wisps of cloud – that orderlies compare to cotton, baker boys to meringue-tops – by the marsh-sun to the west, over the sea that has spread out the freshly ironed tablecloth so a streak or crease is nowhere to be seen.

If you smooth out a tablecloth you imitate God.
If you set the table for one you imitate God.

HEYDAY

in underwear woven from tree branches
I arrive in the evening of this blessed day
on seductive bedding, *tiger,* if you dare

the day actually began at the swimming pool
in a swimsuit braided from birch
that bore unripe bud-buttons

on my nose rested glasses carved out of
leafy stalks as I read through
a manuscript about girls in pink dresses

pink balloons floated across the sky
as I looked up and out the window

no one appeared in the doorway with orders for an arrest
before I left for the theatre
in an evening dress made of twigs

wore a necklace threaded with earthworms
around my long and thin neck

the handbag made of ink
socks of saliva
high-heeled basalt shoes

WE DRINK COFFEE AT A KITCHEN TABLE

white kitchen table and a radio on a shelf
the open newspaper gives the order of the day:
today we think about chlamydia, black death, and tuberculosis
we lift the coffee cups to delicate lips
snow falls heavy in the stillness outside
the backs of our hands are decorated with faint freckles
the sun touched us a few times

we love you day, we love you morning moment
thank you for allowing us to wake up

a young man died in Hollywood last night

we close the paper and turn on the radio

if Eros himself came here he'd feel faint
at the sight of such well-groomed hands
and send us lovers forthwith
but his majesty has never visited Iceland

we drink the coffee

ODE

the muscles got tired of holding up
the eyeball, spared me seeing
myself grow old, mature on a pan
on the stove of time

the idle tongue in the hollow of my mouth
I liken to an unemployed puppy in
a dog house

it strokes the inner walls
strokes the inner walls
like a home-crazed rag

before, it appeased, pacified, kissed
now others will whisper
say something nice; or nasty!

as a maiden I rose from a long sleep
in a green reed, or blue, in a lightless girlhole
I met a mirror that deep-voiced said:
'see your beauty!'

later it drew me a yellow line on the floor:
'come no closer!'

but white are my teeth
saliva soft as a spring

and the first hairs that sprout on my grave
are plucked by the girls on the lower corridor
laughing with the pincette

we girls also laughed as we
pulled weeds in the public park

girls laugh

time took me by surprise

recently a young woman led me up
steep steps
she is my mirror image without quicksilver

how old is my embrace today?
my breasts – x minus eighteen years old?
my lips?

my kisses?

that reminded some of absinthe drink
others of a stream in the morning

how old is my breath today?

the moments that I lived
fight over my bones
like the last breadloaf in a famine

does the vulture eat its own carcass?

and the lad on the night shift
rearranges and rearranges
invisible pictures on the wall

of mum
of children
of a minke whale
that, bloody, arrives at her wedding

a streak of blood on a long skinny fjord

the armpits of the lads, who on the beach
open the bride with man-sized scissors,
bawl with rage

and what I remember as I tore the membrane
off my bridegroom
with long, colourful nails

under the window in the midday sun
out in the dining hall, over a light blue tablecloth
is a quiet sweat pearl falling down my forehead

it is the superglue, strong as glass,
that fixes me to the ground

so I don't rise from the grave
muttering nonsense
like a newly graduated high school student!

warm blood
runs through my veins like wine

though some call me the waste in the sieve
I produce like a fountain
juice for adult diapers

the freckled wasteland on his arms

that rearrange the pictures
that sprinkle the graverims with water from a jug

I see more clearly than my own reflection

look!
how the mushrooms dance
in the forest behind the material world
when the girl touches you
with her eyes with
her moist lips

A MARRIED COUPLE DRINK COFFEE AT THE KITCHEN TABLE

the coffee maker is new
these are the first two cups that we drink
of the coffee that she prepares, bought in honour of the day:
forty years since we married at the city magistrate
that same night we drank beer
and played around with the camera
arranged all kinds of tableaux
now it's time for this one

SUNDAY POEM

crooked grows the heather
and a single twig
on the pubic hair
of the soil

damp waits the soil
for luggage
for fodder

Beneath a paved sidewalk lie two giantesses
side by side without touching but the smoke
from their breaths, or a slow fire,
is braided together above the chimneys
on the square that boys and girls on
skateboards glide across.

Leather-clad fathers of daughters who use
perfumes rich in sunlight and live far from
the square – who bury, meanwhile,
their dolls in the garden – stand
by the motorcycles and eat
sugared pancakes from the shop.

Those of us who rose from the dead
sit on the benches, hold ice-cream.
A leggy dame strides across the square.
Now rings the phone of a girl dressed in black.

She answers and takes leave of her brother:
'Emergency call! Yet another man in mortal danger!'
Her brother is the friendly boy
in the shop, the one who's always waiting for some action.

Militantly she steps into the black carriage.
'Quick,' pleads an anguished man on the phone and
sees in his mind's eye his mother making a joke,
falling back with laughter – the image refreshes,

inspirits, and improves the ill; a classic last resort:
echoing mother's laughter.

The street that the anguished man lives on was erected from paper,
he moved here to be buried alive.
A sweet death for placid people but in the interim
he just gets these terrible fits – by a
sketched garden gate the emergency vehicle skids
silently: the tyres are soft as skin.

It wasn't a moment too soon: the pressure
inside would have in the coming minutes torn apart
the abdomen. The girl lays balmy hands
on the trouser fly and softens with
delectable medicines the life-threatening fire.

Diagnosis: *white blood clot*.

In other words: *emergency milk clot*,
which kills if a woman does not churn out
the organ's painful blockage in time.

'You have cured me!' shouts the man.

She adorns her nakedness with her foremother's next-to-last-century bodice. On her wrist she has tattooed two names, her cat's and her mother's. Her hair is pink, straight, shoulder-length. She loves someone, something, feels it inside at times. Her toes plump, arches high, short-legged, wide ankles, her blocky fingers touch beautifully another person's flesh.

If only mum knew how well she touches a man. If dad knew how well she touches a man. Like a tailor touches scissors to velvet. Something happens in her fingertips near a man. Something like a virtuoso near her instrument. So it goes.

With her child on her breast she sits on her mother's coffin, who from the inside kicks like mad at the unpainted veneer, but isn't allowed to come out just yet: 'Relax, mummy.'

Her father makes himself comfortable on a rose-pink sofa, touches lightly a rifle resting on his skinny knees while his twinkling, dreamy eyes watch a silent television.

Outside the sitting room window the evening gale moves like a metronome the hanging birds that the father shot.

The girl takes the baby from her breast that reminds the cheerful of a satchel of wine, shakes the kid, lays it on her shoulder, stands up, walks about.

Who was it again who taught her to wash herself down below? she thinks. Her accusing glance searches for the culprit who taught her nothing at all.

It is thanks, then, to the higher powers that she knows how to love a man so well. The pride fills her with a comfortable purpose. Her hips soften the square sitting room: the presence of a woman in the home is oft worthy of thanks.

The father scampers to the coffin, produces a handkerchief, blows his nose, produces a key, opens the casket. Sits down in his seat and looks expectantly at the television.

The lid lifts open: the mother in the casket sits up. Her hair tousled, her appearance vulgar, primitive. She is large-boned, surprised, wearing the black dress, stares at the father and daughter and grandchild, but without help she can't get up; thanks to the hip.

The doctor will call as soon as the ship with the plastic hip arrives. Then he will carve himself a piece from the old hip, whittle from it teeth for his lady-love; he beat the others out. The damage must be mended though she has never kissed better. 'What are teeth for, anyway?' asks the doctor who now knows that nothing is as it seems: so ruined hips, too weak to climb out of coffins, can be put to use. That's what teeth are for.

The new-fledged mother cried the other day at the doctor's such fair tears that he desired to acquire, to make glue for the postage stamps for the letters that he, in old age, plans to send his wife – his second, he loves her most of all. *Young women cry beautifully at the doctor's*. And if only the tears of a girl who mourns the sickly hip of her mother were to make their way into his funeral shroud!

'Would the new-fledged mother give the doctor a tearspecimen for the sake of science?' The girl dried her face, said she couldn't bear to lose her mummy. He promised that mum would live for many years yet with a plastic hip.

'If you allow me to stroke your tears with a swabbing-pin I will take great care in the hip operation and use the finest nails for the fastenings,' the doctor offered the girl.

She immediately consented to the taking of the specimen. He would split the tears between two test tubes: *pink* and *green*. One for the glue under the postage stamps, the other for the drops for the crotch of his death-briefs. Happily would he die with an erection.

Note:

It is said that if men die with erections they go to heaven, directly home to the lovecastle where an endless celebration prevails. The grapevine encircles the bunk beds and the saliva tastes better than champagne.

'Your mum is not going to die. She will see your children grow up, inherit and echo our stupidity. That I promise you, young lady,' reiterated the doctor, prescient.

She who will bear witness to the collapse of generations sits upright in the coffin and asks for help getting out.

The daughter pushes her mother down into the coffin, lays the grandchild in grandma's arms, closes the casket, locks with grandpa's key that she then sticks between her breasts, leaves.

The mother kicks just once from the other side of the panel after the front door closes. The father in the pink sofa blows his nose into a crackling-dry handkerchief.

The wind revs up so the hanging birds outside increase their tempo. The car is started, accelerated.

'My days of youth went something like this, little one, if grandma remembers correctly,' she whispers to her grandchild as they lie, the two of them in the coffin. 'I was happy with play and work, had a hula hoop, scooter, sports socks, trainers...'

Hours later the girl comes home, opens the casket, picks up the baby like a treasure. She offers her mother a trusty and sturdy hand and pulls her to her feet.

'You are pretty mum, a real knockout.'

Grandpa is asleep on the sofa. His friendly fingers that have smoked cigars and loved women hold the rifle delicately.

She tethers her mother and child to a chair. Brings them a can of fruitmush.

'Well mummy dear, now I'm going to paint the casket.'

from

SPIDERS IN
SHOP WINDOWS

★

(kóngulær í sýningargluggum)

2017

KEEPSAKE

the mirror seizes my image as I handcomb my morning-pink hair
and locks the image in a cell, the toothpaste is striped
        yellow
        blue
        white
        red
        ugh –
my soles are lonely and supple [sickly]

HERE WITH US
THOUGH NO ONE / NOTHING BELONGS TO US

glittering orbs rotate in the air
tearbeams glimmer on the walls
distressed monkeys rotate on their tails
a tear glistens on a cheek
a tear glistens on a cheek
the street lanterns outside blink the greetings of the deceased
    who refuse
        of course
to show the living the path
oh
there is no path

     do I sense the floral scent of thy pores
     venerable judge?

oh
there is no path

     do I detect the filthy stink of the words
     the human stench of the shadow?

oh, there is no path

a child sleeps on a trampoline – a sister dreams of a water slide
a child sleeps on a trampoline – a sister dreams of a water slide

there is no path

glittering orbs hang in the air and call forth shadows on the walls
the moon rotates in a spiderwire
there is no path

street
lanterns
hang
their
heads
electricity
drips
down
the
corners
of
their
mouths

TUG OF WAR AS I SLEEP IN A MOONSAND

the moon pulls up
the earth pulls down
the moon up
the earth down
up
down

    *

I lay down on the sidewalk and fell asleep
I awoke, stood up
I awoke, stood up
I awoke, stood up
lay on the sidewalk, fell asleep
lay on the sidewalk, fell asleep

    *

after careful reflection on decorative mobiles, pairs of shoes,
    a pendulum, earth, sun, moon
the police officer moved closer and cut

       horizontally

    the vertical
    rope
    in two

       a thump

a horizontal
vertical
thump

the sound takes shape before my eyes, thought the police officer
as the corpse
dropped
onto the floor and didn't set the earth quaking

down
down

up
up

down
down

up

ADVERT

glassbreasts
glassbreasts

THE COLOURS IN MY DOLL'S HOUSE

the floor is pale green
the walls are tinfoil
the sofa is pink
my tongue green
my eyes holes
an unfamiliar human leads me from the room

SEQUEL

and the evening took off its head and offered it to me and asked me
    to take care of it and
comb its hair
it's good to sleep
said the evening while I combed the locks
be happy every time people show your sleep interest and listen
if you say :
my gloves are missing

AROMA

this pink night ignites the butterflies that fly outside the window
the flames lock their claws into unsaid sentences and cats' eyes
    magnify your image
that projects onto the dreamscreen while the cars in the cinema
    make love at the garbage heap
at daybreak the lovers catch fire

        do you smell the aroma of rust, lubrication,
        sentences, soil without damp?

while you blink your eyes more butterflies and more butterflies
    catch fire
while we blink our eyes

        do you smell the aroma?

cat tongues comb the curls and the eyes magnify the images :
we will dance on naked envelopes

LAUGHTER

the sky opens its mouth and swallows a cloud
    cloud
    cloud
    cloud
    oh
the sky is truly hungry
and laughs toothlessly between bites

I lie down on the ground
               mmm
and laugh with the sky
            mmm
laughter

I've been aware of Kristín Ómarsdóttir for as long as I've considered myself a poet. She is, no doubt, a *grande dame* of Icelandic poetry – but among my generation (at least) she is also something of a cult figure. I have a poet friend who has made it a rule, every time she meets Kristín at an event, to lead her directly to the bar where they raise glasses of cava. This – besides being a devastatingly covetable relationship – is exactly the kind of thing one imagines happens to Kristín Ómarsdóttir.

My perception of her has always been that she is driven first and foremost by the work, and not the fanfare. This is an important precedent to set in Iceland, which is a small pond full of big fish, where doing mildly interesting things and getting a whole lot of attention for it is something of a local delicacy. But Kristín's artistic trajectory demonstrates real integrity; for over three decades she has consistently produced work that is singular, striking, and strange, and has done so without courting pop-cultural idolatry.

Because Iceland's book industry relies so heavily on the Christmas gift market, in which the product must above all be new, contemporary Icelandic literature regularly and as a matter of course goes out of print. As a result, the only way to get hold of the majority of Kristín's poetry books for this translation was to turn to the library. This experience was a sobering reminder of the importance of making work accessible – continuously, to each new generation. While a variety of forces influence the shaping of a canon, publishers certainly play a significant role in preserving and bolstering a writer's reputation and readership. They do this not only by keeping their books in print, but also by taking care in their presentation – the ways in which books are edited, designed, and printed are aesthetic choices that can have decisive implications for a writer's legacy.

I recently heard Andrew Motion describe Ted Hughes as '[coming] at the subject like a bull at a gate', and it reminded me of the violent and imperialistic attitudes that poets can perpetuate through the aesthetic choices they make in their work. Kristín's poetry is especially refreshing in this respect. Her poems shift nimbly between subjectivities: the lines demarcating gender and family roles, and defining personhood and points of view, are fluid. In our final round of edits, Kristín asked if we could change the son in one of the poems to a daughter, and I simply couldn't object, not even for the sake of historical accuracy. Shifting the subject between genders, without warning or qualification, as the poem itself shape-shifted between languages, felt faithful to her poetic ethos. Strict as I was about everything else – I am, to all intents and purposes, a literalist when it comes to translation – this edit felt like an internal homage, true to the spirit of her poem 'scissors', which invites us to 'grow together not apart':

> cut a piece from the eyelid of a son or daughter
> and sew into one's eyelids
>
> [...]
>
> old gets a new one, new gets an old one
> a son gets a father's, a mother a son's

But what we choose to talk about is just as important as how we talk about it, and Kristín situates us firmly in the domestic realm – we are in the garden, the kitchen, the bedroom, sometimes as far as a hospital or café, but always seemingly close to home. In Kristín's hands these everyday scenes and backdrops take on heroic proportions. There is a kind of domestic mysticism at play in her poems, which are imbued with an element of fairy tale, of the Germanic variety, with all the attendant brutality and violence. One feels in many of the poems the incessant 'tick-trickle' of threat, and indeed there are as many rifles in her work as there are kitchen stoves and coffee cups. This setting, the seemingly mundane everyday imbued with a constant threat of violence, is, as it happens, the lot of every woman in the world. And yet, despite being attacked from every angle, women and their domestic experiences are rarely deemed dynamic enough to be the stuff of serious literature. Kristín, meanwhile, invites us to consider the struggles of her heroines in terms that are as urgent, as close to life, death, the divine, and the sublime, as anything we might know from fairy tale and legend.

Eavan Boland has described how the 'chronicling of interiors' by painters 'revealed the intimacy of the attachment between the body and its immediate horizon'. She asks why poetry has not been allowed to do the same, why

> poetry's historical sense only came alive when it left the house? What did it mean for generation after generation of poets that the world outside was deemed to be a horizon of moral transcendence and pastoral significance? But not a half-empty cup, a child's shoe, a crooked patch of sunlight on carpet?

What Kristín's work suggests is that the topics on our 'immediate horizon' – family, love, and sexuality among them – are not simple givens, not one-dimensional subjects sufficiently plumbed, but in fact more complex, mystifying and perhaps mystical than we are encouraged to believe. 'If you smooth out a tablecloth', one of her poems says, 'you imitate God.' I repeat this to myself like a mantra, combing through her words day after day for weeks on end, trying to find their English sons and daughters. 'If you smooth out a tablecloth you imitate God. / If you set the table for one you imitate God.'

Vala Thorodds
Walsden, West Yorkshire, 2018

NOTES & ACKNOWLEDGEMENTS

I would like to thank Kristín Ómarsdóttir for entrusting me with her words and giving generous and insightful annotations, being forthcoming and kind throughout the process. Thank you also to Luke Allan, my first and last reader, for believing in and encouraging this project from its inception and for being the finest editor in England. Many thanks also to my amma, Þorbjörg Þóroddsdóttir, for allowing me to spend many hours at her dining room table in Garðabær working on this book, and for taking a great interest in the project, resolving queries about some of the more formal language.

The capitalisation of titles in the table of contents and on the section title pages reflects the original texts. Likewise all idiosyncrasies of punctuation have been retained. In a few cases, with the author's approval, the italicisation of speech and similar elements has been adjusted in order to establish consistency and clarity.

'Fire' ('Eldur') was an existent alternative title for the poem 'Þórukonuljóð', provided by the author. In 'Nightpoem of the Washer-up', the subject was changed from 'son' to 'daughter'. 'Quatrain' was originally three lines long and bore the Icelandic title 'Staka', which can mean either 'Verse' or 'Quatrain'. The poem's lineation was adjusted so that it ran to four lines rather than three, in order to accommodate the preferred English title. Again, these changes were made in agreement with the author.

'Napoleon's hat' buns (p. 103) are Icelandic marzipan pastries shaped to vaguely resemble Napoleon Bonaparte's bicorne hat.

spiders in shop windows is a sequence of poems rather than a collection of discrete works. Though the entire sequence could not be included, the selected poems are presented in their relative sequential order.

Icelanders have patronymic names and are thus always referred to by their given names, even when using honorific titles, hence the reference simply to 'Kristín' on the cover and in the editorial material.

The book's epigraphs are from Sasha West's poem 'Agriculture Begins' in *Failure and I Bury the Body* (Harper Collins, 2013); and Lauren Elkin's *Flâneuse* (Chatto & Windus, 2016).

The translations in this book are based on the following first editions, most of which I checked out of the Reykjavík City Library in Grófin (all but two being currently out of print): *Í húsinu okkar er þoka* (self-published, 1987); *þerna á gömlu veitinga-húsi* (Mál og menning, 1993); *Lokaðu augunum og hugsaðu um mig* (Mál og menning, 1998); *Sérstakur dagur* (Mál og menning, 2000); *Jólaljóð* (Salka, 2006); *Sjáðu fegurð þína* (Uppheimar, 2008); *kóngu-lær í sýningargluggum* (JPV, 2017). I would like to acknowledge that in the process of translating this book I paid the equivalent of about £36 in library late fees.

In the afterword, Andrew Motion's comment about Ted Hughes is from his conversation with Paul Muldoon on the *New Yorker* poetry podcast of 19 April, 2017. Eavan Boland's comments about poetry are from *A Journey with Two Maps: Becoming a Woman Poet* (Carcanet, 2011).

A few of the translations in this collection have appeared in *Granta*, *PN Review*, *The Guardian*, *The Penguin Book of the Prose Poem*, and *Pain*.

Thanks to Art Omi for hosting me and Kristín in November 2019, allowing us to revisit these poems and make revisions for the second edition.